The Life and Times of Nostradumbass

Bernard Christophe

THE LIFE AND TIMES OF

NOSTRA-DUMBASS

BY BERNARD CHRISTOPHE

Illustrated by Tom Morse-Brown

Library of Congress Control Number: 2012912835
ISBN: Hardcover   978-1-4771-4542-5
                 Softcover   978-1-4771-4541-8
                 Ebook   978-1-4771-4543-2

This book was printed in the United States of America.

To order additional copies of this book, contact:
Xlibris Corporation
1-888-795-4274
www.Xlibris.com
Orders@Xlibris.com
111280

I would like to thank all the people who helped make this book happen. I appreciate you both.

Tom Morse-Brown: I could not have done this book without you. Thank you for sharing your wonderful gifts with such a gracious heart.

CDP II: Thank you, thank you. Your knowledge of Middle Ages history is amazing!

I would like to dedicate this book to my wife Lucille and our twelve daughters. You know who you are.

1

First of all, it's pronounced Du-mas.

My father was French,

but don't hold that against me.

If you are reading this though, you must have

somehow stumbled upon my writings,

my musings, my thoughts, my prophesies,

my, ah, my stuff.

Most people are familiar with my older brother,

Michel Nostradamus.

He's actually my half brother.

To be honest with you,

I'm not even sure which parent we share.

Don't ask.

Mickey (as I call him) is the one everyone knows.

He's the famous one,

the one everyone wants to be around.

Michel... the great prophet,

Michel... the answer man,

Michel... the all knowing.

I'm quite sure Mary and Joseph's other children

understood a bit of how I feel.

Okay, maybe a bit more.

It is true that Mickey's an incredible person. I won't

deny that. He always has been.

Mom used to say,

"He was born thirty years old."

When I asked her how old I was when I was born,

she just gave me a long knowing stare.

I guess I must have been pretty young.

Mickey was always a little different than the

rest of us kids.

I remember when the gang would be outside playing

kick-the-oil-lamp, Mickey would be locked away in

his room, huddled over his books and writings.

The guy never took a day off.

Once I came in and asked him if he wanted to come

out and play with the rest of us.

He just sat there.

Then, ever so slowly,

he turned his head, and with barely a glance in my

direction, he said, "Do you think pain, misery, death,

and destruction ever take a day off? I think not!"

Needless to say,

I never asked him to play again.

2

Being only two years apart, we used to compete in

everything. Of course, he always won. Whether it was

Greek, Latin, Math, or even pre-American history, he

always came out on top.

Well, not in everything. I was actually a better singer.

He hated singing.

He used to say that singing would give him a "joyous

sensation within my bowels, one in which I

cannot endure."

His words. I know... kinda weird.

I think he just didn't like feeling happy.

For me, though, singing became my escape.

I remember as a young boy, I would gather together

the dogs and cats, even the farm animals. I would

throw my head back, and with everything within me,

I would begin to sing.

Oh, how I loved to sing. From the very depths of my

soul I would bring forth song after song, spontaneous

in their composition yet aged in their meaning.

Though, by the second verse, I would usually be

standing there alone. I was confident my furry friends

were with me in spirit.

People would ask me all the time what it was like to

follow Mickey through school.

Year after year, it was the same thing.

Upon finding out that I was Mickey's brother, the

teacher would drone on and on,

endlessly describing in detail how wonderful he was.

"Your brother was so focused,"

"Your brother was such a studious and responsible

young man."

"Your brother this, your brother that."

Finally, around the time I was twelve or so, I couldn't

take it any longer.

From that point on, at the beginning of each

school year,

I would walk into my new classroom, introduce

myself to the teacher, and before he could say a word,

I would say,

"Just so that you know, I am nothing like my

older brother. I know I will probably start out

as a disappointment to you, but because of my

lighthearted personality and my unhealthy desire to

please, you will come to enjoy my presence in

your class." Sure enough, they did.

School didn't turn out to be so bad after all. Of

course, Mickey was awarded

"Most Likely to Succeed."

That was a no-brainer.

But I ended up getting "Class Clown." It had a few

perks at first (the ladies dug me), but soon enough, I

saw the downside; it boxed us in for the rest of

our lives.

Mickey pushed himself harder and harder to achieve

great things (which he did), and I, well, I ended up

expending great energy trying to make people laugh.

That may sound like a noble endeavor, but in this

recession we're in

(we've started calling it the Dark Ages),

it made for one tough audience.

It's hard doing knock-knock jokes when people are

actually locked behind their doors with the plague.

I mean, I would literally go door-to-door knocking.

It was tough.

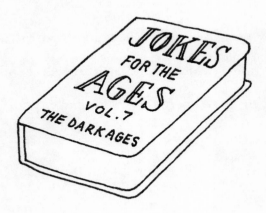

3

Needing something more to do, I began to

spend more time with Mickey, hoping to pick up

something, anything, just from being around him.

When I asked if I could join him in his study while

he wrote, at first he said no. Eventually, though,

he relented.

I guess all that knocking finally paid off.

Mickey allowed me to enter if and only if

I said nothing and sat quietly in a darkened corner.

I looked around the room.

To be honest with you,

every corner was darkened.

It wasn't called the Dark Ages for nothing.

Watching him was fascinating.

He would sit and stare at a candle, often for over

an hour.

He said that it sometimes took that long to empty his

mind before he could begin to write.

Then suddenly, he would grab a pen, dip it in the ink,

and like a man possessed, he would begin to write.

Often, during rainstorms, instead of a candle or the

fire from the fireplace, he would stare intently at

the newly formed yet tiny rivers that would cascade

swiftly down the hill outside the room.

He used to say,

"I've seen fire, and I've seen rain."

Such a deep well.

For hours he would write, word after word, line upon

line, constantly dipping his pen to refill it.

Sitting in my little corner and watching him write

was, at first, spellbinding.

But after days and days of exactly the same thing,

it got to be a little old.

And not just that.

He would often write and never take a break for food.

Now that's just not right.

When he was finished, he rose, and with nary a word

(we say nary a lot),

he would give me a quick glance and then swiftly just

walk right out of the room.

I was always fascinated by what he wrote.

Being the curious fellow that I am,

I would often saunter over to his desk

and check out his handiwork.

He said they were prophesies, but looking at them,

they never made any sense to me.

Here's an early one:

Century 3, Quatrain No. 22

"In the third month, at sunrise,

the boar and the leopard meet on the battlefield.

The fatigued leopard looks up to heaven

and sees an eagle playing around the sun."

See what I mean? Sunrise, animals, battlefields...

It makes no sense.

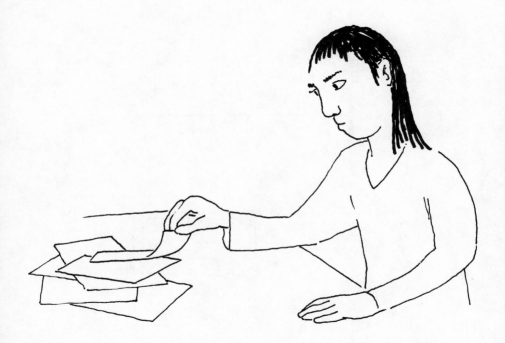

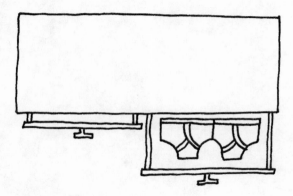

4

Mickey had a unique way of presenting his work.

Upon finishing a new section, he would arrange his

writings in the same exact way. Each small section

was called a quatrain.

A quatrain is a stanza consisting of four lines. Mickey

would write one hundred quatrains and then group

them together in what he called a century.

He's always been organized.

Even as a little kid, his underwear drawer had both

pairs folded and neatly arranged.

Though I saw how serious he was about his writing,

not everyone was enamored with him.

Many would scoff or make fun of him.

The children were the most cruel.

They would often make up their own quatrains

about Mickey,

boldly mocking him to his face.

One of their favorites went like this:

"Mickey, Mickey, writing machine,

all he ever eats is beans.

line on line and row on row,

he's full of gas from head to toe."

Mickey really hated that one. I actually thought it

was kinda funny.

Mickey did have a problem though.

Because his quatrains were so abstract,

one could come up with multiple meanings for just

about everything he wrote.

That became the dividing point.

You either believed him and, therefore, revered him

and held him in awe, or you thought he was insane or

a calculated fraud.

I mean, "The boar and the leopard meet." Seriously,

that could mean anything.

Come to think of it, it actually sounds like our

family reunions. Huh.

His most vocal distracters said, and I quote,

"Nostradamus is one hundred percent accurate at

predicting events after they happen." That's true.

To be honest, they all had valid points.

One thing was certain: no one was indifferent when it

came to Mickey.

Kinda like lima beans.

As his fame grew, leaders from near and far would

travel to Mickey to get their futures told. This

frustrated Mickey at first, but soon, he said

he realized "there's good money in futures."

He said one day that people will actually be trading

in futures.

When I asked him what that meant, he looked at

me, shrugged, and said, "I haven't a clue."

This was the first time I'd ever heard him say that he

didn't know something.

He instantly swore me to secrecy, making me promise

never to reveal it.

So please, don't tell anyone.

5

And so this is where I began my own journey into

writing and forecasting.

Maybe, just maybe,

I could come up with something that someone would

pay to hear.

Like Mickey, I went to my room, lit a candle,

and got my writing implements together.

I would begin to stare at the candle's inviting flame

and begin the process of emptying my mind.

A few seconds later, I started to write.

At first, things came rather slowly. My first attempt

had me waking up hours later in a pool of my

own drool.

As I lifted my head, I gazed at the image on the

paper, wondering if maybe its shape had some

significant meaning.

I thought it looked like a boar, or maybe a leopard.

That's about the best I could do.

My problem was that I just couldn't get what I

wanted to say down in four lines.

I tried, I really did. Each time though, it seemed as if

I was one line short.

For example,

here's one of my early four-line quatrains:

In summer the winds will blow,

telling you just where to go,

but soon will come fall

bringing change to it all.

Agh! It just seemed one line too short.

Then it hit me. Mickey's quatrains were all just four

lines. Maybe I could one-up him and add a fifth line.

And guess what? That's exactly what happened.

I invented the five-line quatrain.

But now I had a dilemma.

The word quatrain, used to indicate a stanza of four

lines, would no longer work for a five-lined stanza.

I now had to come up with a new term.

It just so happened that my cousin Richard was

visiting from Cannes, a quaint little town in the

south of France. Cannes was known for an annual

event called the Cane Film Festival.

Each year, cane makers would show off their updated

cane designs with new filmy coverings that was

supposed to make the canes last longer.

I went once as a kid. Not too exciting.

Anyway, Richard had a bum leg.

He told people that it was an old war injury, but

the family all knew it was a result of a game of kick-

the-oil-lamp gone wrong.

Watching him limp by one day, I decided to call my

five-line musings after Richard.

Instead of a quatrain, my five-line prophesies would

henceforth be known as a limp-rick.

Most in my family thought I came up with the name

because I'd overheard Richard's wife use that as his

nickname after their honeymoon.

The family always laughed about that, but I never

really got their little joke.

6

Life was now beginning to change for me. That extra

line I added was all I needed.

Limp-ricks flowed from me like part one of my

morning ritual.

One after another poured forth

until after the first month, I had almost three.

I decided I would stand in the town square and

recite some of my limp-ricks for the townspeople.

They were actually very polite as they continued to

walk by.

One of my early favorites went something like this.

Well, it actually went exactly like this:

Limp-rick No. 3

There's coming a prince from Paris,

who'll want to marry an heiress.

he'll search through the city,

for one that is pretty,

and finally end up with the fairest.

I know, at the end, instead of an s, I added a t.

But give me a break, it was one of my early attempts.

I was hoping Limp-rick No. 3 would catch on with a

local prince who was ready to settle down.

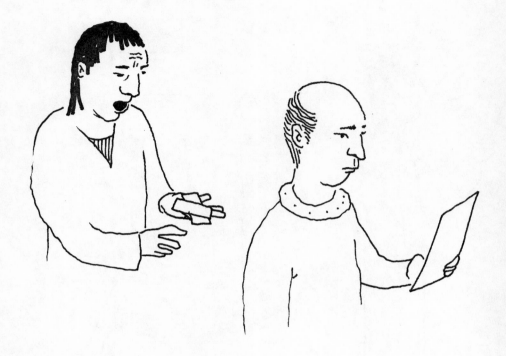

Maybe he would even want to buy some futures.

Well, sure enough, there was a prince who bit.

He was getting on in age (he was over forty), and he

needed a little help with the ladies,

so he paid me for the prophecy and went on his way.

Good luck, old man.

As you can imagine, I was now a certified professional prophet. People began to call me the bomb. No one knew what the word meant though. So I decided to look into the future and bring forth its meaning.

I decided that the word bomb would become something that people would use to bless each other. It would be a good thing, a useful tool to humanity that would celebrate life, especially for families.

I know, I know, it's amazing. I can actually see things that "will be" with the clarity of "what is."

I even amaze myself.

7

One day, Mickey announced that he was in love with

someone named Henry.

We all thought that odd since that was the king's

name. Upon further explanation, it turned out that

her name was Henrietta.

That seemed to make Mom and Dad a bit happier.

Henrietta was a lovely young woman, but she always

seemed to be a little sickly.

Oh, that stupid plague.

She and Mickey had two wonderful children, but no

matter how deeply he delved into medicine, he could

not help Henrietta and the kids.

Sadly, they too joined the throngs of victims of that

terrible sickness.

Mickey became distraught beyond belief.

Here he was, the great prophet and healer, and even

he couldn't save his family.

As you can imagine, his prophesies became more and

more morbid. Each one seemed to top the last one

in pain and misery.

So many focused on the end of the world.

Soon, everyone was reading into his prophesies and

picking a date when the world will end. Will it be

1600, or possibly 1776? How about 1929? One even

suggested December 2012. Idiot.

As my brother's writings became more depressing,

my own limp-ricks took on a more whimsical tone.

THE SUN WILL PROBABLY NEVER SET ON THE FRENCH EMPIRE

Maybe it was the old class clown coming out in me,

but I felt that the world, mired in the darkest of

times with a deathly plague hanging over

everyone's heads, needed something that was more

positive and uplifting.

You know, like candy for the eyes.

Here's one that came during that time:

Limp-rick No. 14

New lands will arise on the earth,

as France increases her girth.

The sun will not set

on the lands she will get

while the poor Brits will never give birth.

It seemed very easy to see a future

where the French (and not the British) would

eventually rule the entire known world, very similar

to the ancient Roman empire.

It would be much less violent

(we are the French) and would, of course,

have considerably better food.

Ah, a world full of lovers and fine dining. Come on

now, who wouldn't want that?

I just felt like France needed a good shot in the arm.

Again, I'm not sure what that means, but it seems

appropriate to say.

I know, I know, I'm amazing.

8

As the years passed, my brother Mickey began to

get older. Again, my observations are spot on.

Fortunately, he met another woman

(a rich widow named Anne, lucky guy), and together

they had six kids. Boy, did that ever change him.

Oh, his prophecies were still pretty morbid,

but they got him outside to play kick-the-oil-lamp.

I saw him smile three times during those years. It was

a beautiful thing.

In 1566, his gout, which had bothered him for

years, became much worse. It looked as if his days of

prophesying were over.

He called me to his bedside and drew me near.

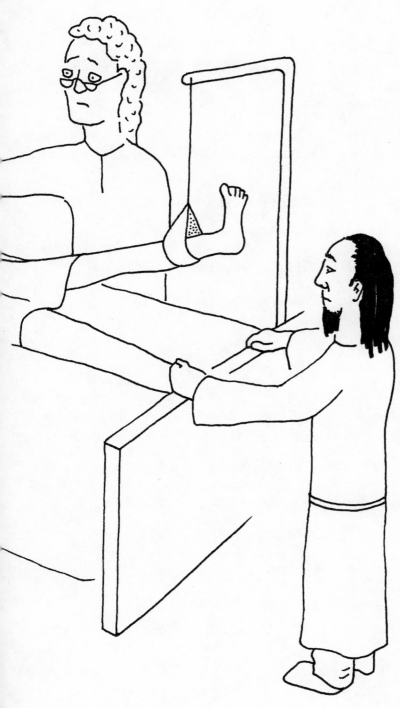

Though his family and his secretary Jean were there
(what's she always doing here?), his words were meant
only for me.

I have never uttered Mickey's last words to anyone.
They were stored in my heart, and only now, after I
have passed, will others know what he shared in secret
with me on that fateful day.

Mickey softly put his shaking hand on my face,
coughed, spat in a bucket, wiped his face, coughed
again, wiped some drool, and then, with a stone-faced
gaze, looked into my eyes and said,
"Dumbass, you've been almost like a brother to me.
I will die soon, and there is no one left to carry on my
work. No one, that is, except for—cough, cough—
except only—cough, cough." And with that, he fell

back on his bed, a lifeless look plastered across his face.

I began to weep.

Wave after wave of loud anguished cries poured forth
from the depths of my soul. Mickey sat up and said,
"Quiet, I'm trying to sleep. Oh, and by the way, I'll
be dead by morning." He was right.

By morning he was dead.

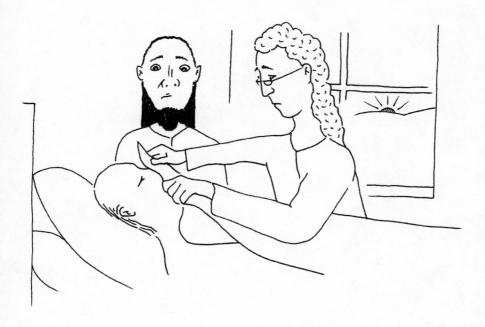

Right again. Agh! Even in death he has to be right.

Though we were French, we held an Irish wake after

his death.

It only seemed right.

9

Mickey was gone, and now, only I remained.

I alone was left to carry on the name.

I gathered his family and asked for his writings.

They looked at me and said,

"With all due respect, Uncle Dumbass, there is no

way you're ever going to get Dad's writings."

And so, in keeping to their word, I didn't.

I did get one of his pens though.

It wasn't in the will. I stole it from his room.

As time went by, people began to look to other things

for guidance and security.

Borderline legit prophecy seemed to be on its way

out, and science was becoming the next big thing.

I felt sorry for all those folks who believe that the

earth is round

(people down south would be falling off if it was

round. Won't they ever get it?)

or that the sun does not revolve around the earth.

Such silly people. They'll come around.

For a few years I kept at it, but eventually, I realized

that it was futile.

Not only was I running out of things to say, but

when Mickey died, no one even considered to listen to

me anymore.

That's when I remembered those words from my

mother just before she passed away. She turned to me

and said, "Dumbass, Mickey is your meal ticket.

Stay close to him. By the way,

I'll be dead by morning." She was.

I've lived a very good life, but I must admit, I look

forward to a time of retirement and rest. I think I'm

tapped out as far as prophecies are concerned.

So how does a great prophet like myself rest? I'm

glad you asked.

I would love to travel the world. I do love to sail.

I had a friend when I was younger named Jacques

Cartier. He sailed to a faraway land called Canadanada

or something like that.

He built a state park somewhere close by. Very nice.

I also thought about heading east to visit Mr. Ming.

He owns a dynasty somewhere in China that makes

vases and other breakable objects.

I hear they're a peaceful bunch.

Then I might visit Spain. I'd love to travel along with

the Spanish armada. They're a fun group.

But in reality, what will I really do?

Probably nothing.

I'm really a homebody if you must know. I have

all these great ideas of going here and there, but in

reality, I'm too old to travel.

I'll be sixty-seven on my next birthday. They do say

that the sixties are the new seventies.

I'm feeling older even as I write.

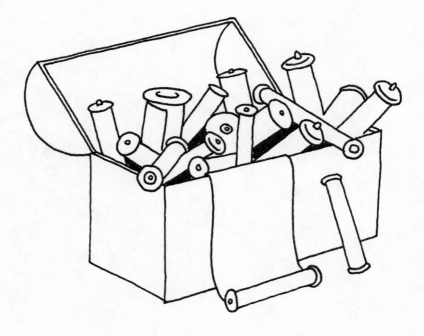

10

If you are still reading this (God bless you), then you know that I have already passed away. I mean, I'm not dead at the moment. Well, at you're moment I am, but not at my moment, that being now... for me.

Mom said I had an amazing gift to confuse even the simplest of things. She truly was the wind behind me, or something like that.

I have left alongside this historical treatise a scroll containing the complete collection of my limp-ricks. I think I have, oh, let's see, about 7,238 of them. But who's counting?

Mickey himself had a couple thousand quatrains. Fine attempt for sure.

I hope that history will be kind to me and that my

writings will reveal to all

my true depth as both a person and a prophet.

I think my mother said it best: "When people really

get to know you, they'll discover that you're an inch

thick and a mile wide."

She was always so encouraging.

I loved my mother.

At least, I think she was my mother.

Don't ask.